SOMEBODY GIVE THIS HEART A PEN

SOMEBODY GIVE THIS HEART A PEN

SOPHIA THAKUR

CANDLEWICK PRESS

First US paperback edition 2021
This edition published specially for Five Below 2021 by Candlewick Press
First published by Walker Books Ltd. (UK) 2019

Library of Congress Catalog Card Number 2020915496
ISBN 978-1-5362-0992-1 (Candlewick trade hardcover edition)
ISBN 978-1-5362-2296-8 (Candlewick trade paperback edition)
ISBN 978-1-5362-2484-9 (Five Below edition)

21 LSC 1

Printed in Crawfordsville, IN, USA

This book was typeset in Adobe Garamond and Fjalla One.

Candlewick Press
99 Dover Street
Somerville, Massachusetts 02144

www.candlewick.com

Save your heart from its silence.
That corner of you wants a poem.

Contents

. . . the process

Before place, before time.
Before God separated the water from the skies.
Before factories, before machines, before money, before screens.
Before the internet, before iPhones. Before you and before me.
It was vacant.
And from this empty all there was to do was grow.
And so we did. And then we waited.
We waited to see how things would unfold.
We listened to how many stories were told.
We watched and saw how things could flow,
how they could change
and they could burn.
How things got better while things got worse.
So we began to pray and we learned to break.

We broke to let the light in. Broke to let it out.
Broke and waited for the right thing to fill tired skins out.
We broke to break and broke to heal. Broke to feel alive
and broke to just feel. Broke to humble and we broke to build.
Broke to take. Broke to give. Broke to forget and broke to fix.
From fixing we learned and from learning came life.
Came reasons to go and more reasons to try.
But more than that, from breaking we know that though
we shed, we can always regrow.
Always reseed.
Always restart.
This is the natural process of a heart.

This book mirrors the process.
The building, the breaking, the learning and recreating.
Your skin turns inside out.
Each limb becomes a heart.
Bloody body parts across plain paper.
Find some *I*s to dot and *T*s to cross
until the mess resembles poetry.
Read yourself between pages.
Learn to speak heart.

sugarcane is sweetest at its joint

if a child washes his hands, he may eat with kings

it takes a village
to raise a child

wood already touched by fire is not
hard to set alight

a wise man who knows proverbs
can reconcile all difficulties

it is better to walk than curse the road

medicine left in the bottle can't help

laugh at the end

an axe does not cut down a tree by itself

GROW

if you can walk, you can dance;
if you can talk, you can sing

no one can uproot the tree which God has planted

where you will sit when
you are old shows where you
stood in youth

when you stand with the blessings of your mother
and God, it matters not who stands against you

dubeŋ ñinilaa niŋ fitiroo benta

the searcher for the shade will make the dusk

other people's wisdom
prevents the king from
being called a fool

rising early makes the road short

around a flowering tree there are many insects

Somebody Give This Heart a Pen

Try it all at home.
Try it at school
At university
In the office
On the corner of the street that your father lives on,
you never visit.
Beneath your lover's window
next to the years you left there.
In the shower
to your song
Inside the rain
Under the sun
Inside the night
Between the days

Try to find space to hear what your heart says
Make it your best friend
Slow down and clock back into yourself

Give your heart a pen.

Picking a Name

Ignore those scared by your potential
Those who snigger while you figure your path
Ignore when they try to bring out the past in you
What matters is not what you are called
But what you answer to.

Rise to You

With every tomorrow
and next time
and one day
and soon come
the sun grows tired of our waiting,
our excuses and entitled patience,
our confidence in the second chance
that forever holds us from taking one.

What if one day the night never comes
and the sun holds the sky hostage
and *acted-upon aspirations* are the price to pay
for night to ever come again?
How many twenty-fours would it take
to give action to these ideas?

Pump action into you
whether it's making that call or making that plan
the sun shines brightest on those who stand.

Excerpt from a Letter to My Little Black Girl

Little black girl, my heart thrives in the stride of your halo.
The moment you stop considering yourself
a collection of cherry-picked stars,
my ribs bury themselves into my back and I fall flat
against the earth's concrete that was built for YOU to fly from.
May the soles of your Kickers or the flats of your Dolly shoes
act as an atlas to navigate this wilderness.
Run your fingers through your Afro,
a tree that this whole culture breathes from.
Blue Magic drops, like diamonds, glistening,
adorning your skull.
Liquid gold dances down your neck because our mothers said
that we must always over-oil.
That this British weather wasn't made for us.
Yet Britain was paved by us.
Leave Out seeping through the pavements,
yet waiting to be straightened by those who harbor
frustrations over assimilations instead of celebrating
cultural integration.
Leave your Leave Out, baby girl, we're making space for that.
Leave your hair print on every seat back.
You are art, and we all see that.
Your tones to them are on tanning beds,
and your features are in catalogues.
And your back . . . oooooh,
don't let them shame you for that.
In the West, they try to play you for that.

Try tell you, you affi shake a bit of that.
But baby girl, don't ever let them sexualize your black
in the same breath they will conceptualize your black
to make appropriated crap, and you're too lit for all of that.

One day you may have to work twice as hard,
for half of the pay.
Swerve abuse
with a smile on your face.
But diamonds find such life under pressure.
As a diamond you can't help but shine when you enter.
So see your skin as celebratory.

Beautiful melanin, set you apart.
Beautiful melanin, work of art.

Girl, you better see yourself in that London skyline.
Big Ben is trying to tell you that it's your time.
The London Eye is just a shadow of your Afro
because your face is absorbing all of the light.
You will shine bigger and brighter than the Shard,
your blood runs ten million times deeper than the Thames.
No wonder they've tried to steal your magic.

Baby, you are
the finest collection of stars.
Every morning I'll remind you that this world is ours.

You are the finest collection of stars, for sure.
Don't ever forget that this world is yours.

How She Breathes Now

My mum said that giving birth
is like pulling a part of your heart out
and watching it learn the earth.
She said that there will never be a day
that my pain doesn't add into hers.
She said that her heart has been staining her sleeve
since she had us
and she's probably breathed significantly less
since we came onto this planet.

She said
sorry in advance
for the day that she no longer has anything to add
but her words.

I looked up, buried in eyes—hers in mine—
and said that she's taught me the most precious parts of life.
A lesson in selflessness. How personal needs should bow to love.
A lesson in unconditional.
A lesson in never giving up.
A lesson I will wear on my skin for as long as I live.
A standard of love
which I will both seek and give.
I've seen the Jesus in her.
I've watched her channel God.
She's taught me how to come second to faith
and this has taught me how to hold on.

Mama's Song

Richest mahogany,
skin
stretched, spread and softened across candyfloss cheeks
that eat with the beats of laughter
and fight the fleet of a dimple
after your smile illuminates not only your face,
but the entire room.

Constellations birthed in the womb.
One day you bear fruit to galaxies
seen and adored by the naked eye.
I pray that my son learns to love your kind.
To find in a woman dimes more precious
than anything similar to gain.

My aim is not to inspire
the perfect woman for my son,
but more for my son to align
all that is perfect
with a woman.

I pray that my son never throws shade
on the light rays
within our girls' confidence.
I pray that he takes the time
to take her in as a portrait of the universe
and marvel through the world in her eyes.

Girl, You Better Sing

Baby girl,
Hum Beyoncé and Erykah into the street corners.
Time your steps to the beat
Miss every crack, every weird look and bum note
Hit the chorus under that next streetlight.
Turn and twirl in the arms of it
Let it guide you to feel beautiful
without anybody saying so

Pull your voice from your toes up
Let it grab and hold onto your fear
Open your mouth and drag it out
Let the sound dance down your tongue
into the soft of this evening
into this orange, beating-the-dark sky
that waits for you to get home
before passing onto the cold.
Let 7 PM's warmth explore your skin
Sing
when it's breaking
Sing
till you're shaking
Sing every last part of you inside out
and look down in awe of your wholeness.

Don't stifle that smile
Let it rip through your face
like a postcard into
you
are deserving of such joy . . .

talk half, lef half

a roaring lion kills no gain

he that beats the drum for the mad man to dance
is no better than the mad man himself

faroolu meŋ be naaneeriŋ,

woolu le jiyoo ka bori ñoo kaŋ

sake of mouth, fish get caught

silence cannot
be misquoted

ears hard pikni go to market twice

silence is also speech

the tongue slips and slides

hurry hurry has no blessings

the bell rings loudest in your own home

when two elephants fight it is the grass that gets trampled

even the mightiest eagle comes down to the treetops to rest

WAIT

a tiger does not have to proclaim its tigritude

the one who talks too much leaves his mouth empty

you are your neighbor   *kairo sill maŋ jaŋ faa*

the road of peace is not far, slow slow

i ye i jaatii tara meŋ na, ining a si wooke

he who refuses to obey cannot command

do like your host

those who are absent are always wrong

haste and hurry can only bear children with many regrets along the way

the big game often appears when the hunter has given up the hunt for the day

examine what is said,
not him who speaks

only someone else can scratch your back

it is in silence that the world presents itself

pausing phases

The seasons always simmer into clasped palms
The years fold into our past.
Everything uncontrollable revolves around us
And we try to move just as fast
Competing with stars to burn brighter
And forcing winter to callus our skin.
Obligating our whole selves to finish lines
Forgetting how beautiful things are when still.

Daddy's Accents

I think that my dad left his accent
inside the burning pink cheeks of his law class.
He's dropped pieces of it since,
along the path to assimilation.
It is hard to place his voice.

On Mondays he wears a mask, proving thick and fast
to new clients that as much as he is British,
he is also an expert in his land.
Offering a hand in tearing little Africa to pieces
of corruption and capitalism but promise and potential,
making the young boys dance to the nostalgic rhythm
of a white man's wallet on arrival.
He has had to learn every rope intended to hang him,
to discern which beast is worth a seat to eat with.

He's coming closer and closer to home though.
He spends more time there, and with each trip
he brings back a tiny bit of his accent.
He laughs like a boy with his childhood friends,
and the dining table shakes and trembles at the thought
of what a man with many masks can do.

the leaders won't

Only expect to experience honesty from the view
that this valley offers, overlooking this very moment.
Believe nothing before this point because the leaders lie.
In fact, sink your toes into the sand and anchor here.
Recline into your idealism till you are almost facing the stars,
and count how many parts of the manifesto manifests.
Let the politicians drum dance around your ear
like Notting Hill,
and appreciate it for no more than a great performance.
This valley is the stomping ground. This valley is the blood
and sweat and other building blocks. This valley is where
we see reality, away from the sequined interviews and
colorfully feathered promises. This valley is pre-Grenfell.
This valley is why they really pushed Brexit before leaving.
This valley is Windrush passports in backpacks, gathered at
the bottom with workers' tags and seventy birthday cards,
and Oyster cards and a freedom pass, and probably glitter
because that just gets everywhere,
like we did,
making things glisten under eyes that couldn't wait to see
something different.
They wait for a distraction to move them off in the night.
Joke's on them, it caught a headline.
Joke's on us, it's still happening.
This valley is Damilola, Stephen Lawrence, Mark Duggan.
Void, violent stop and search, kill him if he's running.

This valley looks up and sees the one percent, sending
their wounds down in tax brackets, carefully packaged debt
delivered to our crumbling doors.
I let go of the hills for a second and the sky fell in on us.
This valley is a diamond barely balancing on the fingertips
of the few down there who actually give a damn if we drop.

So give a damn, because the leaders won't.

Fearmongering

Police aren't after conversations
they're after culprits.
They don't sharpen their fangs
for us to feel safe.

He wakes if he's lucky
with bite marks lining his back
branding his black
with empty court dates and arrests made in vain.
Anything to sow shame
anything to make sure he never feels safe.

So of course I ran
I've read this story one hundred times over.
And I'd rather run blissful in ignorance
but alive,
when stopping could be suicide.

The Lessons of Adolescence Are Not to Be Learned at the Border

Only when showers become rain
and ceilings, skies
will we progressively empathize
with packing home into a backpack.

You cried to whichever god you decide
You tried Vishnu, you tried Allah, you tried mine
You tried politics, you tried charity, you tried asylum
You tried robbing things, you tried faith, you tread mines
You tried tunnels, bridges, boats, you toed every line.

You carried your life in two palms
Had to sit and watch them cry
Had to answer all the difficult questions.

Like *Mummy,*
why?

Why are we running from home?
Why do we move in the night?
Mum, why do they hate us this bad?
Mum, why are they full of rage?
Mummy, why are they splitting us up?
Mum, why am I in this cage?

People.

We've seen this before
We've seen the Holocaust
We've seen slavery
We've seen wars
We've seen flawed division govern us
Since before we were born
Yet we refuse learning from these lessons.

We are callusing where we should soften.

God and Politics

Order is sketched into the concrete of my elder's heart.
Never will she depart.
She was a black woman in Russia in the Sixties.
Learning about a politics that hated her for existing.
Her palms were forced to find each other
in the face of everything.
Before anything
there was God and God is love so "let that be your politics"
she pleads with us through every call card,
the most effective repeating record ever heard.
She writes on life inside the lines
she's tried to tread so carefully since her youth.
Every Christmas I want to squeeze her,
arms of acceptance,
and just tell her that we believe her
and we respect her
but I don't.
Or rather I can't
because our grandparents' secrets should remain
as foreign to us as communism
in our perfect, pretty little mouths.
So we let her be perfect, to give this advice.
But what would help more is removing the mask.
I think that I'm remaking the mistakes of your past
and there is more to be learned from the lessons that you lived
than from the proverbs you decorate your lectures with.

Grandma, If You Can Hear

How did you discern between what you want
and what's worth it
How many lessons make a learned one
How did you work out your purpose
How do you shake off a burden
How much of your parents do you become?

Do I plan ahead or ride the wave
Does the world belong to the rich or the brave
How often did your inner circle change
What happens to the secrets that you gave?

How do you know they love you for real
Will I ever love like this again
Does a heart get stronger after breaking
Or do we just get better at pretend?

How does your body get used to losing a loved one
when they die, or when they just leave
or when they stay, but they fade
and forget who they used to be?

When does compromise become sacrifice
When does sacrifice become surrender
What on this earth is worth surrendering to
Do aspirations become disappointed in you
Do you hear them mutter could've beens behind your ears

Or does responsibility become the driving factor
behind any adult's career?

Do you listen to the mind or the heart
to get the right thing done?
Because right now I'm risking
a lot in the name of love.
Before I risk it all
I thought I'd send some questions up.

So hit me up.

With love,
S

Fighting as Strangers

During the second class they asked where we grew up.
Him with the scars scattered like knives across his face
said he came from the desert.
A place where conflict was engraved
into the spirit of man.
Where holding your child was a rarity
that induced a peculiar softness
never to be explored.

They came to me and I froze
because really, where I grew up had never factored
into my growing.
How do you say you were raised in between arguments
and slamming doors.
And you had to grow away from everything you lived in,
to stay sane within four walls?
I'm more familiar with Mum's tears
than I may ever be with her joy.

I learned that *kids* was spelled *leverage*
once differences became more promising
than marriage vows.
I grew up in stagnant divorce
empty-shell exchanges and egg-shelled floors
fake smiles served to guests on the shiniest of silver,
reflections rebounding like spears.
Before dinner they bow their seasoned heads

as the last thing they can agree on
and pray for reason to stay
and the strength to leave.

Whichever comes first.

Love was never brought into the argument.
Funny that the thing that brought them together
in the first place
became undeserving of a mention.
I'm sure it still sits in both of their mouths
buried under a tongue too trained away from togetherness
to ever come up.

I suppose I grew up like him,
with a heart of scars.
Holding tight to a love layered in loss
and that is what has made us who we are.

Wrinkled Time

Are you a picture of too much life,
pulling at threads across your face?
Or are wrinkles wisdom finally trusting you enough
to break into you?

I think the latter.

I think that they are signs of breaking and entering
and your eyes tell me that the years have stolen much from you.
But your Sunday-stained calm tells me that you still own
everything that you need.
Your eyes are tired but satisfied.
Sat there surrounded by the same features that they came up with.
Same mouth that swallowed time, love, hate
and whatever the eyes couldn't take
year on year.

But today it smiles
and pulls joy into the rest of a wonderfully wrinkled face.

His 1,000 Years in 75 with Her

Every night for fifty years before we sleep
I ask what she would like to dream.
We connect satin to skulls, nose to nose,
and make only the things able to touch us our entire globe.
I don't ever want to live on a different page to her
not even unconsciously.
Before I make my way into the night
I get to hear how magnificent her mind is.
We've walked to Venice for lunch with both of our parents
and we've shown them that things can work.
We've sat and watched our stillborn singing,
and in her dream it doesn't hurt.
We have dressed up and danced under the Seventeenth Chapel,
and laid our heads to dream in many a king's home.
We have laughed into our famous friends' houses,
and we have built holiday homes along many coasts.
Sometimes we revisit the one fight that flooded us both,
and she gets sad again and then pulls me in close.
We have made up in extraordinary places.
She loves a sorry written into the Indian shore.
With every year that passes
we head further and further into these dreams
and it softens how far they continue to become

from our aging reality.

Postcard People

I first saw you beside the bar.
You were a gap in the sky
spilling stillness into anyone smart enough
to stop drinking and forgetting
and just take you in.
Your head was low enough for the music to bounce off
your neck
back to the speaker that had rejected it.
You were mixing up your fingers and Rizla
deciding which was created for which.
Which would lift you, which would hold you.
Time set up camp in your pocket.
I became intoxicated by your isolation.
You were here
in the middle of the festival
with a force field of quiet around you.
I'm sure that you didn't even notice the guy beside you
racing to the bottom of his glass.

Someone pushed. You didn't bark.
You took a sidestep to the left and laughed.
And I swear it was as if your cheeks were attached to my
intestines via puppet strings, they rumbled and untied
themselves, broke through better judgement
and pulled me into you.
I had nothing to say but it was far too late,
I was staring at your face wild-eyed and infatuated by you.

And then you spoke
through your smoke
and I swear, all till now, I have no idea what you said
but I'm so certain that light lives behind your lips.

Say what you said over and over again,
may I mishear it each time until I have poems between us.

You are so beautiful, standing there, like frozen light,
observing what we do under this sky
is what I wish I had said.
But I tucked my head into my chest and left
wishing that I could fold all of my secrets into your palm.

That way even if we were to never meet again, I'd know
that some of the most sacred parts of me live and swim
in something so indescribably breathtaking.

beautiful boy

Turns out the last sunset that we all faced
with our mouths as open as our cameras
was just your face smudged against the sky.
I knew I recognized that light.

feather bodies

Wild-eyed,
we dive into each other as the only possible place to go
from here.

Why do these arms not drop into wings when I hold you?
How has anatomy not adjusted to the desire of the heart?
How are two thin limbs all that I have to keep you
from breaking?

My body fails me.

Eyes that can't take in enough of you at once,
lips that can't cover you.

How is it fair
that you have been able to teach the earth my laugh
in as many languages as we have loved?
And you've molded into the safest corner of life
every time it becomes on tops.
And you've been perfect peace whenever I need,
but my body still won't do its job,
to become your soft landing
whenever the world knocks you off.

Foreverlove?

The last time that we were able to love quietly
was the last time I believed in foreverlove.
And even then.
There was absolutely nothing silent about the 5 AMs we
burned through, or the many mornings absorbed into your
windscreen that I learned you inside of, until
each part of my day was stained by each stage of you, K.

Perhaps what I mean to say is,
the last time we loved peacefully was the last time I believed
that if a feeling is able to devour you whole,
it's worth surrendering to.
I, maybe, know better now.
Beasts swallow whole and so does love,
and so do many things in between.

Somehow the smiling scars of what has been
are able to convince me, from time to time,
that I can try . . . maybe . . .
to love you without learning you again.
To see you without having you hurt me again.
Meet you passively, perhaps.

I overestimate the calluses I expected my heart to have grown
by now. I overtrust the independence that our distance
forced me into to activate when I see you,
but muscle memory is stronger than the female empowerment

songs I was singing on the way. This chest sees your laugh
and hears your voice again.
Then we hug and somewhere a firework kisses a sky,
and poles collide, and everything that has been struggling to
connect, intertwines.
Your skin remembers mine and I die to the idea that you
have no power over me.
You think loving is hard?
Have you tried loving and leaving and loving and leaving
inside the same kiss over and over?
Have you sat your heart down and told it to not get caught
up this time?
Have you been constantly disappointed in your mind for
forcing its way back to that place?
That helpless, obsessed, sometimes jealous, never-at-rest
place that always wakes to your inconsistencies.
Heart, *fold*.
For goodness' sake, just give way to the head this time.
It's actually right this time.
Every time you simmer, I see it as the rest of the body being
ready to see him again. And every time I wildly misjudge
my strength and my soft.
Give me discipline from hindsight
and faith in foresight.
One day this heart will see him without softening
and the mind will meet him and not care.

Or is this the love that you fight for?
Is that why this is so ridiculous to bear?

Risky Nostalgia

And as more time sowed itself into our separation
I began to remember the bee for its honey
and bad memories lost their sting
and the wounds assimilated peacefully
and I let them decorate my skin.

Maybe, now,
it's okay to miss . . .
to let think . . .
to become drunk in thoughts of our better days
to call you when emotionally sober
to send a card on your birthday.

Maybe it's okay to tell you that I still love you . . .
maybe it's safe because you said you still loved me too
what harm is there in honesty
maybe it's okay to see you?

Maybe it's okay to kiss you again
and hold you as if you were mine
(I WON'T BECOME NEEDY)
(I WON'T BECOME ATTACHED THIS TIME).

I contemplated flexing the new me when I saw you
but instead tried to offer the version that you knew
before the arguing started
before our final fuses blew

and in trying that, I realized
that I've gone beyond being that woman for you.

Time away from belonging to an "us"
allowed my preferences to become personal again
and really I never liked your sharp tongue
nor the nature of your crew.
These were things that I once contested
and then just became accustomed to.
But since you,
things are less weighty.
I'm no longer waiting
for calls back
and texts back
and affection back
and respect back
and love back
and honesty back
and honestly, in seeing you again
after healing from those pains,
I see right through the me that ever loved you.

I got to know the hold that you had on me so well
the hold that strangled out my expectations
the hold that forced *every single possible coping mechanism
known to man*
to work in the name of our potential.

And after months of balanced emotions
and healing and self-devotion
I tasted it again
that shot of rum in this nostalgia.

There are smells that remind me of nights I'd rather forget
and I can no longer go near those drinks
and while I thought I'd be happy to see you
I tasted the rum on your lips
but this time,
I run.

When the Strong Friend Cries

The happy friend, the passive friend.
The friend without choking emotions.
The friend we roll over, roll onto and roll with.
The friend with both sides, the ears and the eyes,
the one you may walk by because his head's down.
The unimposing, the unprovoking.
He cried when she died and nobody knew.

My guy, take as much of me as you need right now.
Everything for you would be better used,
peel this skin off, wrap it around you
tight enough to hold you together.
And if you still break
when it still aches
if in the night you still wake
and think of her
think of me
I'll try to be everything that you could possibly need.

When God Wept

Angels are throwing fireworks across the night
light is cracking open the cloud
wind is screaming for the balance
that we were meant to find under the sun.

God is roaring
heart opened by his people
who became bigger than the earth.

His sadness shakes the sky.
The moon has hidden.
We all look up
surprised by nature's autonomy
and for a moment we let in humility
and exist in necessary insignificance.

And then the roar turns to rain
and then the day comes
and we become spoiled once again
by nature's grace.

the rain falls on every roof

if you pick up one end of
the stick you also pick up
the other

some people feel the rain,
others just get wet

the person making the bonfire suffers from the heat

the night has ears

anger against a brother is felt
on the flesh, not in the bone

a log never becomes a crocodile
no matter how it drowns

do not let what you cannot do
tear from your hands what you can

BREAK

if all seeds that fall were to grow,
then no one could follow the path
under the trees

the plant protected by God
is never hurt by the wind

there are no shortcuts
to the top of the palm tree

all monkeys cannot hang on
the same branch

a man with a cough cannot
conceal himself

when the moon is not full,
the stars shine more brightly

How We Got Here, Part 20

Love came last
After broken trust
After selfishly protecting our own hearts
After nights waiting for your call
After counting hours before I'd reply
After stalking you online
to find you still talk to her.
After choosing vengeance over communication
After we started tripping over our own lies
After we accepted this as finished for over the eleventh time
After I forgave you again and again
After you realized that I'd always stay
After you stopped trying to impress me
After I stop being impressed
After *he* made me laugh while we argued
After I got bored of you
After you became lazy
and I went crazy
After you hid your thoughts from me
and I stopped feeling secure with you
After comparison swallowed me whole
After strangers showered me with the love you refused to show
After you preferred your boys to me
After I laughed way more with my girls
After I stopped wanting to see you these days
After you stopped deserving the world
After we knew that we could do better

and we settled for affection alone
and then your arms became cold.
After we lost what we were even fighting for
so we just fought
but we were too used to the fight to stop.
After we burned through respect
and aggression met both our palms
After our friends had to mediate
After we stole each other's calm
Stole each other's happiness
Stole each other's space for growth.

After you showed me your true colors
and I finally loved me enough to leave.
After God numbed me to your everything
but I came back to you to heal.
After we started the same cycle again
both knowing that we could never be.

But this war we have between us is familiar
and the comfort in familiarity is easier than either of us
finally finding the strength to leave.

flood

I have been drenched in you.
I'm going about my day soaking,
like us in Canons Park, when your car became a prison
and I escaped to the side of the road and wept with the rain.
That day it understood me where you couldn't.
And held me when you wouldn't.
I'm soaking again.
So of course *you* have pushed your way into every conversation.
Even when I meet those polite folk who only ask with their eyes,
you spill from my mouth like a tsunami.
How vocal this lonely
sliding into every crevice of my day,
I count the minutes by you.
It's been an hour and I haven't said your name.
But still,
there is no getting away from this layer of wet skin
sitting on top of mine.

Where can I go this wet?
Where is quiet enough to listen to the little ripples
writing themselves along my arms,
and then spend hours building those stories about how we would
travel far from here and surf them once they grew into waves?
Everyone leave me alone today.
It's for me and the you of my mind to hold our breath
for as long as possible underneath our reality
which is this.

You have been trying to slide away
through my fingertips as I lay
but you just get absorbed into the sheets
and I wake, flooded in a dream of you again.

What if I let you become a memory?
What if my other organs grow to speak of you
as the flood that almost made them float forever?
What if I see you in every puddle and lake for as long as
we have rain?
Can I ever love again, like this?
Trapped in a memory of the only thing I've ever surrendered to,
with stones in my pocket, eager to have you fill more of me
than these dry bones.

When you left, this heart pushed you up through the eyes for
one million nights
but I still haven't dried.
These organs still float in this flood of you.

How intentional that you should flood,
knowing that the body needs at least sixty percent water.
This means that even when you left
even after the lungs found land
they remained ready to welcome you once more.
I almost wish that you were bad for me,
something that this body would reject.

But you came as everything this heart desired
and for as long as I know this,
really,
you never left.

Whipped on You

There are so many other pockets of life
that are far more familiar than you
that have been so much better to me than you have.

Like these winds that push into my window every morning,
despite being met by closed blinds and complaints,
I couldn't dream of *any* kind of consistent commitment
from you.
But still I lie here, obedient to a lazy morning,
wrapped in this duvet of you.

What . . .
what time did you wake up?
And did you think about me too?
Did you make up scenarios
about the things that we could do
when the clouds clear up
and the skies choose blue
and you always choose me
and I always choose you?

I'm fine thanks, you? And other white lies

We tuck them neatly behind *How are yous?*
Call it protecting us both from ugly truths
Protecting me from being moved
God forbid I should waver from this stone cold
God knows where my insides would leak
To which side of sanity they would seep
To which extreme they would leap.

So *I'm fine* is my stabilizer
Protecting us both from ugly truths
Protecting me from being moved
Protecting us both from being swallowed whole
By a suppressed mood
I'm weary that one day the truth will catch a *How are you?*
And *I'm fine* is beaten by my wild.

By
*I'm dealing with loss and doing a poor job. Of holding it
together and acting on knowing better. I'm permanently lost,
taking old paths, meeting familiar pain, learning a lesson but
doing it again. I was hurt for so long, I think I look for it now
to fill this gap. It's almost comfortable on my skin. I sink into
tears so easily, which is actually great because you can't talk
at the same time as crying. And tears make more sense than
words these days. At least they can communicate the pain.*

But you didn't ask that

You asked about my day

So I didn't say that

I said with a smile
That it's been great.

secrets

Keeping my first was lonely.
I gave her more to keep warm.
I am surprised that my jaw
has not unhinged itself
with the amount of me I keep under my tongue.
My neck has become so tough.

My family has never responded well to imperfection
so the truth of things often comes second.
I swore to my lips
to never send up anything that will compromise
anyone's perception of me.
I have a vision of how I wish to be seen
and I fear that that image will be challenged
if ever they know more of me.

Trust Issues

Sometimes showing love to someone
comes just before being done with someone.
You put your heart in front of someone
but they halve and crush it.
They might've said something that doesn't sit right
or not recognize how airtight
you tend to go about your whole life
but now you're showing them this other side
this vulnerable and honest side
and maybe they don't reply
but they're still active online.
Or maybe they brush by
how broken you became for them
and I don't mean this in a pain sense
more in a lack of pretense sense.
Either way they didn't sense it.
So you think
Perhaps they don't realize that this is me opening
and being real.
So you say it in some other words
and he responds
I hear that, still.
You feel that in your chest and then your head
and then your ego.
Now you can't find rest, you lie in bed
but you're not sleeping.
This stops you from being honest with yourself and other people.

In fact, now you're kind of cold,
closed off and playing games,
not on stripping back a single layer
till you're in someone's veins.
Forcing others to be honest with their expression and pain
knowing damn well you're not getting vulnerable again.

Solanaceae

We blame the night for what we have done
As if the stars inspired our fire
As if we are the tide, and a moving moon forced us to dance
As if the shadows whispered dares into the back of our neck
And we just had to take that chance
To be unapologetic in our mistake making
And joyous in our lawbreaking
And lose as much of ourselves as possible
Knowing that no one will find those fickle pieces of us
In the night.

Club Decoration

You've sipped far too much silence tonight to even smile at anyone
You've imagined climbing into the speaker countless times
To feel as much of something else as possible
Even kill a sense or two or five.
Strange men's lips dance on their desperate faces for you
You've revived your smile from drowning in that glass
Every time you are asked where your friends are.

Truth is, you lost them on purpose
Truth is, watching their intoxication unfold gives you
zombie vibes
Truth is, you just wanted to be left alone
Truth is, the club was the best place to do this
Truth is, we think we come here to chase the wild of the night
Truth is, we are all running from the me version of us
I feel most grounded while everyone around me transforms
Truth is, he was always going to stop as he walked by me
But the gag is, in the cry of my eyes
He'll see what he came here to escape, and keep it stepping
As if I'd reflect his secrets back onto him if he stayed here
any longer.
Truth is, I wear so many optimist insecurities on me,
Even the wind doesn't trust blowing near me
Truth is, it's never taken the dark of the club for me
To dance through my demons.

I've emptied myself into a troubled mind too many times
To trust that if I do it dancing
The thoughts won't still pry in the morning.

Slow Sky, Move On By

Lingering an extra lifetime above only my head
why won't this day end?

It's been 3 PM for six hours
the clouds are hardening
the wind has dropped to the ground
and I'm seconds away from doing the same.
I just want to go again, already . . .
I want to wake to a forgetful sun
I want to leave this afternoon where it is
and rush the night along.
I want to feel as close to the darkness as my skin
and slide right into 2 AM
so I can cry and hurt in peace
until I empty myself to sleep
and then wake, maybe better
but probably wishing this poem over again,
by 8 AM

Scary Everyone

Things are glazed with concern today.
Everything scares me before I meet it
conversation feels like an attack on my space
compliments look like broken promises already
and promises are itching away at my skin
eager to scratch up disappointment.
That hug felt fake.
I don't think that they meant it when they said it.
Doubt is louder than reality
nowhere is far enough
my ankles are anchors
the skin tips of my fingers are prison gates
I want to stretch out of me
I want to crawl into my headphones and hide myself.
Everything scares me today
My hair hasn't sat on my skin since morning
as if it is waiting for someone to tap my shoulder
but the hand is lingering centimeters from my arm
and I've been holding my breath all afternoon.
I woke with a lump in my throat and it just hasn't left.
If someone pushes me too hard
I might dribble down myself like those people made of
Skittles on TV
collect my own head in my legs
let it lie there for a while,

unpick the lump in my throat
talk down the anxiety
because tomorrow we absolutely must go again.

Fidgeting

To you, the silence in this stillness is to be endured
not experienced.
It scratches at every anxious bone that you own.

Do you find peace when you are alone?
Or do you claw your laptop open
chain your eyes to your phone
trade your thoughts for someone else's?
Too busy to impose
on yourself for a moment.

Be with yourself for a moment.
Be yourself for a moment.
Airplane mode everything but yourself for a moment.
Be for a moment.
Don't speak for a moment.

For a moment embrace nothing but you in this present
as the most important something to ever exist.

Cutting

Those arms are the diary of your life so far
Those lines tell me more than you ever would.
But those spaces between them,
those not so bad parts,
must become your focus for good.

This one was rejection
The past aching to make it past your lips.
And this one was no protection
He took more than you could give.
That one was a fatherless youth
That one was various men fathering you
This one was heartbreak
This one was school
This one is the deepest cut
This one is still a wound.

This one doesn't ever really heal.
She looks up and points to her chest.
But she has recognized where the healing must start
and that's often the hardest step.

Let Hurt

Sometimes
to heal once and one time only
first we must properly hurt.
To understand the sadness that stifles us
we must let it stifle us first
let it sink its teeth deep into our eyes
and let whatever leaks out purse
its lips against our cheeks
like a kiss asking us to be patient
to slow dance with the aching
to understand its twists and turns.

So cry in the shower
accept that everything that gathers by your feet
might come from your face
and confuse your sadness with the rain,
then let them both wash away.
But first
Let it . . .

Shiny Black

Breathe. Wipe. Breathe.
They did not mean it. *Breathe. Wipe. Breathe.*
Maybe they did. *Breathe. Wipe. Breathe.*
Miss didn't say anything. *Breathe. Wipe. Breathe.*
They're just kids. *Breathe. Wipe. Breathe.*
You're too sensitive. *Breathe. Wipe. Breathe.*
Well, so is skin.

"Itty Bitty Titty Committee"

They were never flat until Jordan composed a chorus of
laughter from the boys' changing room which sung its way
onto the football pitch that hosted what I hoped would
have been their first outing. Except clearly it wasn't. Clearly
these almonds of puberty were closer to my ribcage than the
pitch, and now everybody knew this.
Knew that *tomboy* was more than a mindstate. That it sat
deep in my anatomy. That evening I went home and played
the drums on my chest.
Beat my heart into making a decision: in or out.
A decade later I still ask, in or out. But not for Jordan or the
football pitch, but for a complex that I should have never
grown. I jumped off a boat in the middle of the Pacific
when I was twelve and parading this sand-dune torso has
always felt like that decision.

Fairground Lenses

My nose is bigger than
My lips are smaller than
My makeup is less than
My hair is thicker than
This hip, this curve
This waist will not satisfy me
These legs are in transition
My abs need to look like hers
We have stopped looking through our own eyes
and put someone else's first.

My body was once better than comparison
but other images of beauty have long stained my eyes
and I can't help but plaster potential over every part of me,
and see much of my anatomy as space to rectify,
forgetting how it felt to look myself up and down
and be at the very least,
satisfied.

Tender

We need to be more gentle with ourselves
we need to heal
we need to explore our sensitivities raw
we need to feel.

Mutuality at the Funeral

Sorry is the greeting of the day.
Nobody talks Gambia, or politics, or the weather.
Those pleasantries are not relevant today.
Not even between strangers.
You follow the sound of weeping
and squeeze somebody's cousin.
Whose is unimportant . . .
Pain is shared
perhaps not halved
but definitely shared, today.
Someone's shoulder tells you
that it's okay to break.
Someone's hand tells you that we will all be patient as you do.
We let ourselves cry
We hug long and tight
We look for words
But nothing fits right
Nothing but goodbye.

Mam Jemma. *Alexander.* Annabel. Uncle Peter. Aunt Fanny.

Foreverdeath

Death, pregnant on her tongue
too thick to swallow past casket throat.
Don't cry
she insists,
talking to her weaker self.
Don't cry
she insists,
talking to her stronger self.
Don't cry
she insists,
talking to any part of her willing to connect with her skin
which has hovered a few centimeters above her body
as if hung by a hook,
held by God
who plays puppeteer
every night for us,
lifting characters from the stage one by one,
which is fine for the play.
But when the lights go on and the curtains open,
and that character is not present for that final bow,
the play doesn't feel much like a game anymore
and the sudden infinity of death weighs heavy
like a funeral beating on your chest
dancing on your lungs to the cadence of forever.
But the indigestible side

The paradox of life is that it ends
despite how well we live it.

Over 365 days I lost two friends to cancer.
Upon burying the second one
I stood behind his mum in shock
that death of the flesh continues lasting.

Death,
it remains in a state of happening.
The only place where faith can feel so failing
but somehow the most natural part of living.
You die a bit more with every second.
For something so gradual
it sure knows how to set fire to the stage at the end
of the night.

This stanza isn't for closure
or anything that will round this feeling off,
it's just hard.
All the time we ever shared is all we will ever share
and I don't know how to tell the lump in the throat
that hopefully this is the last time cancer will have us both
by the neck.

Heavy World

When your world is full of worries
fears
overbearing parents
burning ears
poor choices
followed by loud voices
and not that much space left to breathe

find me.

When you're not feeling your world,

come into mine.

**no man fears
what he has
seen grow**

do not look where you fell,
but where you slipped

bend the tree when it is young so
when it grows old it will not break

**the one who asks questions
doesn't lose his way**

you do not teach the paths of the
forest to an old gorilla

wisdom is like a baobab tree, no one
individual can embrace it

GROW

the strength of the crocodile is in the water

not everyone who chased the zebra caught it,
but he who caught it chased it

rain beats a leopard's skin,
but it cannot wash away its spots

rat no dey

AGAIN

born rabbit

the house roof fights with the rain, but he
who is sheltered ignores it

strategy is better than strength

boto kensengo buka lo no

an ant can never
hurt an elephant

habakkuk 2:2

the sun never sets
without fresh news

from God

Hold on a little longer, I'll find you
I've seen how life is trying to ride you
I've seen your oceans be taken for rain
and how personal you've become with pain.

Not only were the prophets first rejected
but they were exiled
they were tested,
but they still lived in their truth while contested
and eventually their season came.

The right scout to the right game,
the right photo of the right face,
the right time, the right place.

But to first be found is to be great,
is to excel in your lane
is to stay treading your ocean
until they see the rain.
Become a puddle
a pond
eventually a lake.

Keep your eyes on your reflection
and by that, I mean the sky.

You are but the limits that you've chosen to live by.
Nobody promised a smooth one
so let these lines remind you
to hold on a little longer,
the right light is coming to find you.

Nature's Grace

Thank God for every new sun
that lets us find our feet again.
Life's lessons are heavy, and yesterday your shoulders
became weak again.
But forgiveness and healing linked up and traveled through
the night for you,
two predicates of time that will forever ride for you.

So get up
and shed yesterday's skin,
under a brand-new sky is the perfect place to re-begin.

The Groove

You might scream
and you might cry
but as the night falls in
you will dance carelessly in front of watching eyes
wearing a dress that couldn't complement your skin more
if it tried.
Yes, you have been broken
but girl, you still know how to work it.

Sprouting

When you look for me again,
I hope that you become tangled in the jungle
that I planted in the holes that you dug through my body
while I stayed.
I hope you become trapped face up,
to see how beautifully those insecurities can transform and bloom
under the right sun.

I hope you soak in the right sun.
I hope it humbles you.
Maybe one day, by accident, you'll take a sip or dip
in the river that healed me. And in swallowing,
taste all of the things that could have killed me,
but instead, helped me grow into everything that you swore
I could never become without you.

This growth is not for you or in spite of you.
In fact it stopped being about you once I let go of you.
But I'm healed enough to be honest.
It did take being emptied by you
to reseed
and to bloom.
So I guess this is me thanking you
for forcing me to move.

DIY Romance

Tonight is about me
my eyelashes and my time.
My interest, my fashion, my humor and no guy.
I've told myself to be ready by nine
but if I'm late, I'm worth the wait
so even 10 PM is fine.
I'm putting on a show for my showerhead
and surfing my skin with scented oils
I'm getting lost in myself in the mirror
I'm accepting myself as royal.
I'm loving every selfie
exploring every angle of my face and gasping
I'm strapping heels up to my knees
and rising into myself without asking.
I'm thoroughly enjoying how high I tower
above a version of me that would wait
to find worth in somebody's son
finally asking me out on a date.

Soul *Mate*

Friendship is its very own love story.
It stretches past first periods to first kisses to first homes.
It wraps itself around first and second
and every broken heart
tying together the fragments of ourselves
that we let spill into our friends' palms.

A friend makes a moment a moment,
textures the memories of our past
with laughs
with loss
with dance
with trust.

Long live the friends who stayed longer than lovers.

The growing insignificance of blood
when once strangers become sisters and brothers.

(Chon-Tahl)

In heavily urbanized eyes
she still believes in gardens.
In hills a lifestyle away from us
that sit with a soft sky
and watch this city burn but never ash
over and over like wick wrapped around and into the soul
of every speaker.
She believes in music.

Have you seen it?
How it curled her hips
how it melted her limbs
how it filled her throat
how it taught her hope
how it plays God and father
and lover and friend?

I wish you the hills,
the lights, plenty skies, many nights, infinity reasons to dance
and music that forces you to feel it.
I wish you sound that will hold you whenever you may need it.

Making Mum

I told my mum about my day by accident, forgetting that
she picks jasmine and makes her own oil and she picks at
the gaps in my morality, brings it to a boil and lectures me
for all eternity.

Mum made teeth whitener from lemons on Sunday. Since
she started going to the wrong church, she finds new ways
to channel God. What makes you more like the Maker than
creating? She's still looking for Him in her inventions.

We've got these cyclical conversations that we engage in
where she tells me how to be a wife one day, and I tell her that
I'm not even dating.
And she asks why I'm waiting before we engage
in routine debating
over her reality and mine.
Over borrowed time and body clocks. Babies and dream jobs.
Her real world was decorated with a different ease.
A twenties that didn't desire money or degrees,
but my dad, her hand and then my brothers and I,
a superhero mum and a Stepford wife.
This was her timeline but I don't think that it is mine.

I spoke too soon when I walked in.
The day's hiccups forced themselves up from my tongue
and before long my ears were buried in the Bible.

Proverbs were pulled apart and used to patch my mistakes
into clear-cut sins.

She lectures as passionately as she cries.

She lectures as if I am wringing her torso for jasmine oil
and she'd sooner lose breath and die before watching me dry.

She lectures as passionately as she cries.

She lectures as if she is leaving,
so I listen, knowing that one day she will.
And I'm going to need to recreate her by her wisdoms
so I allow everything she creates to spill.

Athletics

When my oldest athletics coach wrapped winter fingers
around bonfire biceps and dragged me to the side of the
track halfway through the drill,
I imagined him holding a woman.
I wondered what he sounded like when he spoke using limbs as lips.
When he forced no space between the railing and my back,
I wondered what else he was passionate about.
Was he a candles man? I wonder.
I wonder how heavy his fist will be on my cheek.
We are — *one candle could burn both our noses* — centimeters apart,
and we are both screaming. I only hear saliva,
and what I thought was about to happen.

Let me back on the track, are you all right?

In a volume older than my age.

Allow me, let me do my drills.

I pull away, he pulls back.

GO inside.

NO, I'm fine.

Sophia, GO inside!

Yo, I said I'm fine.

Sophia, GO inside and then come back.

Then to the cubicle door I cried.
For over the hundredth time,
the athletics track cubicle reminded me that the body's limits
are lower than the mind's.
I thought that only I could see my period.
My mum has assured me that it was to be kept inside of my
legs, mouth . . . it was mine. So why . . .

Why did it sit on my gray tracksuit bottoms, like a stamp?
Why did it escape me, like a statement?
Why did it shame me?

I begged my mum to collect my gym bag from the track
and told her that I'd meet her by the car.
But she is a mother of two boys before me,
and shame has never been an excuse for lost apologies.
I remember once she made my brother and I
wear one T-shirt because we refused to share our food.
Try sharing flesh, she said.
Try manners, she said, before marching me back down to the track,
tail and tissue tucked between my legs,
head low, low voice.

Thank you, Charlie. I'm sorry.

Chestnuts

A chestnut leaves its shell
ready to reflect every aspect of life
including light.
I suppose if I lived within spikes for some time
I would also want to absorb all that can be met by the eyes.

One of nature's many offerings to our learning life
is that some things must be born in hard, sharp shells
to grow to shine.

They fall when they are ready,
glow between chestnut tree leaves and soil
catch eyes
provoke surprise.

I collected you as a child
because you stood out
I collect you now because I understand,

The wait
The weight
The sharp places we learn to be firm in
The often painful patience of learning
I'm growing my fair share of chestnuts
Hard lessons
And their partner pains

The things that I could never coax you to say
The opportunities missed
Wet cheeks while I pray
For this chestnut to drop
And expose the purpose in this pain.

For a season, there will be many hard and sharp lessons to learn
I know this
I've been collecting chestnuts far too long
to not accept this as the process.

Journey of Mirrors

Post—
whitening creams and flawless-finish foundations
these stretch marks and scarrings become confusing.
Should I be refusing my skin?
I loved this scar on my lip when I was small.
It made me feel like a warrior. Sometimes it still does.
I've always seen stretch marks as synonyms for growth
and isn't growth the beautiful part of change?
A woman I know calls her stretch marks by each of her kids' names
and that is still the most beautiful story I've ever read.

Our bodies are God's canvas
decorating time.
Really, it is a privilege
to wear what He writes.

Torn Apart

Not curvy
Not juicy
Not bouncy
At most,
almost.

Sewn Together

Put your ears to my chest
Hear how growth sings
Hear my wounds sew themselves together
with new promises to their skin.

When to Write

When your fists are ready to paint faces
When there is nowhere to confide
When your skin lingers high above your bones
and you're so out of touch with self,
Write.
When the mouth fails
and shyness strangles
and your throat becomes tight,
Write.
When your eyes won't dry,
Write.
Before you fight
Before you fall,
Write.
When they lie to you
When they hurt you
When they leave you,
Write.
And if they return
And they have listened,
You better write.
When the urge arises
Step out of the shower
And write.
When the world denies you
Find your power
And write.

When they speak of a freedom that doesn't include you . . .

Write away those bars
Write together your scars
Write around your wounds
Write into your womb
Write upwards
Write inwards
Write through and write around
Absolutely everything that tries to steal your sound.

Acknowledgments

God, you did that. Thank you for trusting me enough with other people's stories.

Nina, you gave me a poetry book with a Post-it Note under the cover that read, "I hope this book has everything you're looking for." I don't know how you knew that those 101 pages would not only save my heart, but also lead me to write this collection.

When you commit to stretching your heart across the outer planes of your body for a year to feel absolutely everything needed to write a book, friends say be careful; family gather towels at your feet to catch whatever spills.

Chantal, you are closer to a sister than you are a friend. When I first opened myself up to past pains to bring about poems such as "Let Hurt" or "Foreverdeath" and sent you a video of me in tears with the caption "it is written," you put on a cape and many hats and saved me from becoming lost in each stage of this book. More than that, throughout life you've encouraged me to explore my many corners, and I don't know what this book would have become without that wondering.

This book is a record of the people I've experienced life with: you have always been the real poetry. All I had to do was watch and feel to write. Mama, if your consistent grace and charisma aren't already a poem, then this thing that you're holding is not a book. Thank you for being so easy to admire. Daddy, you fantastic man, you've sown the discipline that a mind like mine needed to complete a collection such as this. I hope that you are proud of me. Latir, Jai — my extra arms. Thank you for being the constant reminder that what happens internally matters and deserves to be made external. More than that, thank you for being amused by my constant externalizing.

Cheers to everyone who gave me something to write about: Alexander Paul, 293, Selly Oak, Mill Hill County, an ex or two, home, Gambia, London, Isabel, Sam, Micaiah, the Christians, summertime, winter, friends new and old. Every single story I've ever liked or been told. To everyone who walked with me while I opened myself up to swallow the world: Jane, Krystle, Laurissa, Rosi, Walker Books, Candlewick Press, Crystal, Suli, Yomi, Anthony, Rhael, Laiana, Daniele, Jude, Amani, Yara, Lov, Kojo, Litty Committee, Kenny, Sam, Salma, Shagufta, Afshan and, more recently, Raphael and you.

Thank you for seeing something in me that I'm still trying to recognize. I hope you see it in me forever. More than that, I hope you give yourself some poems — look at how many you've given me.